FINGERPICKING
ENYA

Arranged by Larry Beekman
Thanks to guitarist Jim Giddings for his help in proofreading these arrangements.

ISBN: 978-1-4234-8135-5

HAL•LEONARD®
CORPORATION
7777 W. BLUEMOUND RD. P.O. BOX 13819 MILWAUKEE, WI 53213

In Australia Contact:
Hal Leonard Australia Pty. Ltd.
4 Lentara Court
Cheltenham, Victoria, 3192 Australia
Email: ausadmin@halleonard.com.au

Visit Hal Leonard Online at
www.halleonard.com

INTRODUCTION TO FINGERSTYLE GUITAR

Fingerstyle (a.k.a. fingerpicking) is a guitar technique that means you literally pick the strings with your right-hand fingers and thumb. This contrasts with the conventional technique of strumming and playing single notes with a pick (a.k.a. flatpicking). For fingerpicking, you can use any type of guitar: acoustic steel-string, nylon-string classical, or electric.

THE RIGHT HAND
The most common right-hand position is shown here.

Use a high wrist; arch your palm as if you were holding a ping-pong ball. Keep the thumb outside and away from the fingers, and let the fingers do the work rather than lifting your whole hand.

The thumb generally plucks the bottom strings with downstrokes on the left side of the thumb and thumbnail. The other fingers pluck the higher strings using upstokes with the fleshy tip of the fingers and fingernails. The thumb and fingers should pluck one string per stroke and not brush over several strings.

Another picking option you may choose to use is called hybrid picking (a.k.a. plectrum-style fingerpicking). Here, the pick is usually held between the thumb and first finger, and the three remaining fingers are assigned to pluck the higher strings.

THE LEFT HAND
The left-hand fingers are numbered 1 though 4.

Be sure to keep your fingers arched, with each joint bent; if they flatten out across the strings, they will deaden the sound when you fingerpick. As a general rule, let the strings ring as long as possible when playing fingerstyle.

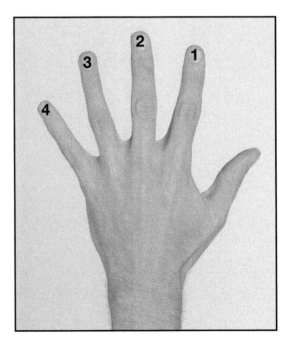

Anywhere Is

Words and Music by Enya, Nicky Ryan and Roma Ryan

Intro
Moderately fast ♩ = 100

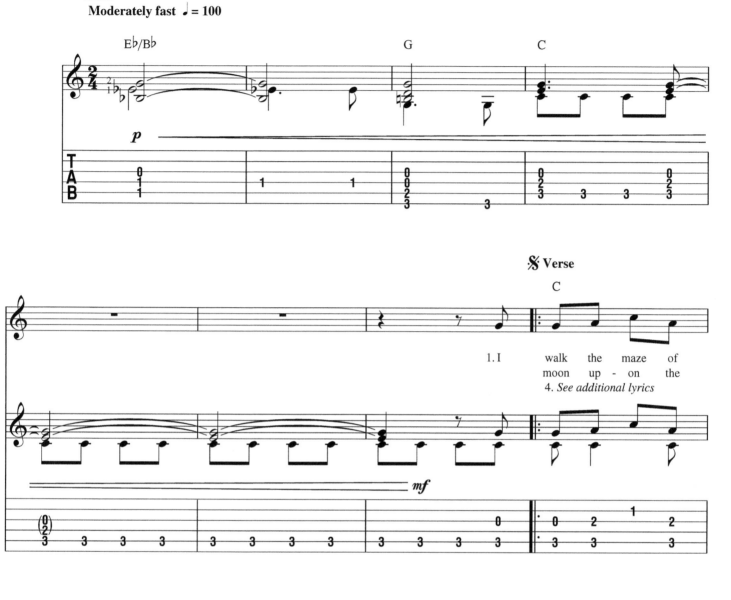

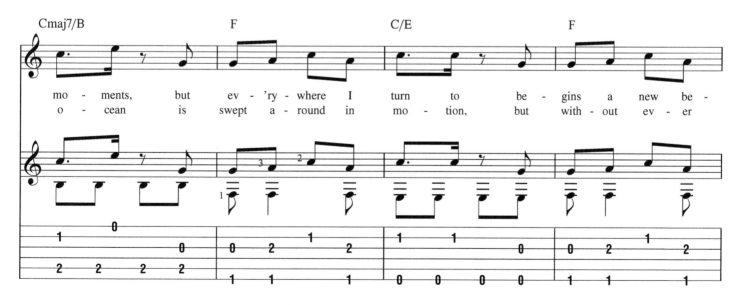

gin - ning, but nev - er finds a fin - ish. I walk to the ho - ri - zon and
know - ing the rea - son for its flow - ing. In mo - tion on the o - cean the

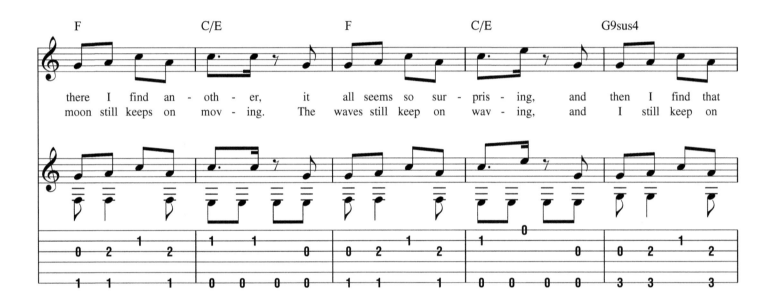

there I find an - oth - er, it all seems so sur - pris - ing, and then I find that
moon still keeps on mov - ing. The waves still keep on wav - ing, and I still keep on

Chorus

I know. _
go - ing. ___

You go there, you're gone for - ev - er. I go there, I'll

lose my way.___ If we stay here we're not to-geth-er. An-y-where is.___ 2. The

3. I won-der if the stars sign the life that is to
5. To leave the thread of all time and let it make a

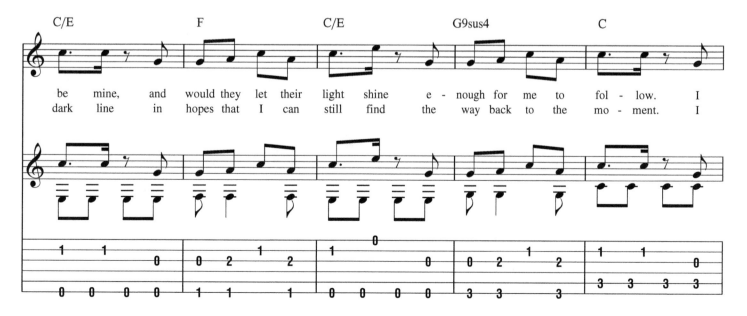

be mine, and would they let their light shine e-nough for me to fol-low. I
dark line in hopes that I can still find the way back to the mo-ment. I

look up to the heav - ens but night is cloud - ed o - ver, no spark of con - stel -
took the turn and turned to be - gin a new be - gin - ning, still look - ing for the

To Coda ⊕

la - tion, no Ve - la, no Or - i - on. ___
an - swer, I can - not find the

Interlude

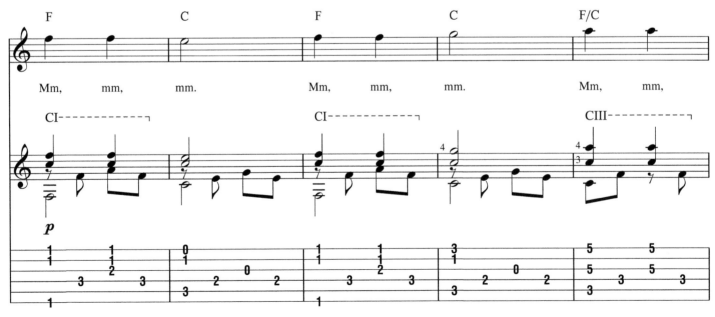

Mm, mm, mm. Mm, mm, mm. Mm, mm,

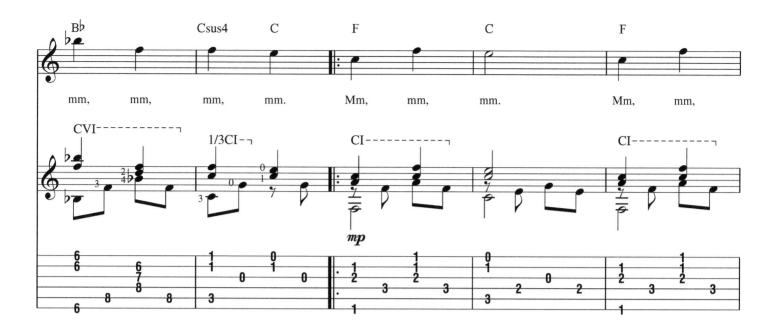

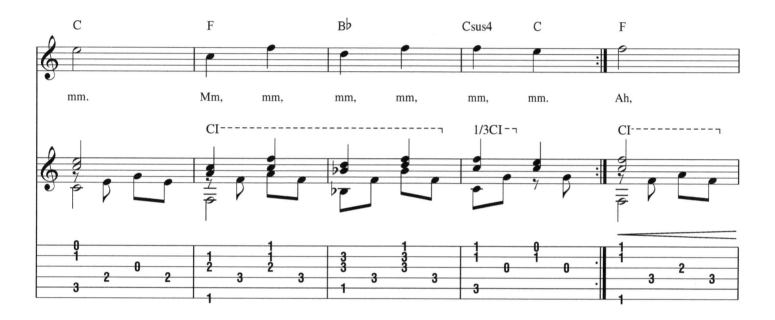

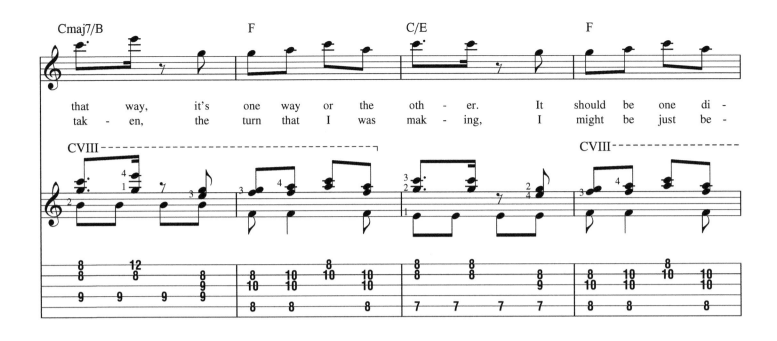

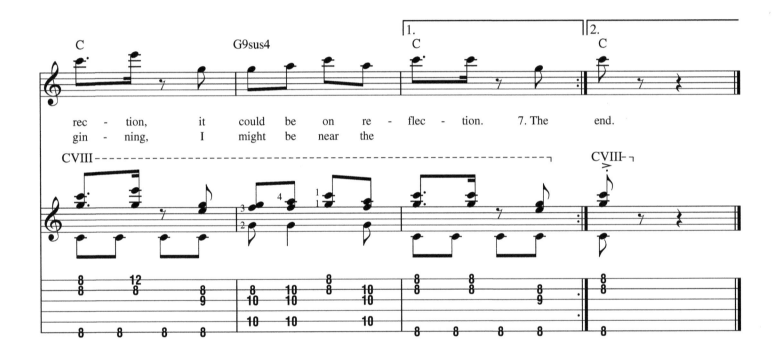

Additional Lyrics

4. The shells upon the warm sands
   Have taken from their own lands
   The echo of their story,
   But all I hear are low sounds
   As pillow words are weaving
   And willow waves are leaving,
   But should I be believing
   That I am only dreaming?

Athair ar Neamh

Words and Music by Enya, Nicky Ryan and Roma Ryan

Drop D tuning:
(low to high) D-A-D-G-B-E

Caribbean Blue

Composed and Arranged by Enya and Nicky Ryan

Drop D tuning:
(low to high) D-A-D-G-B-E

Intro

Fast ♩ = 152

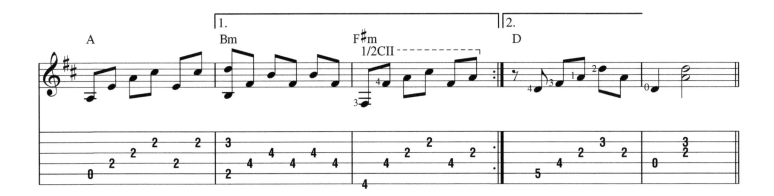

Interlude

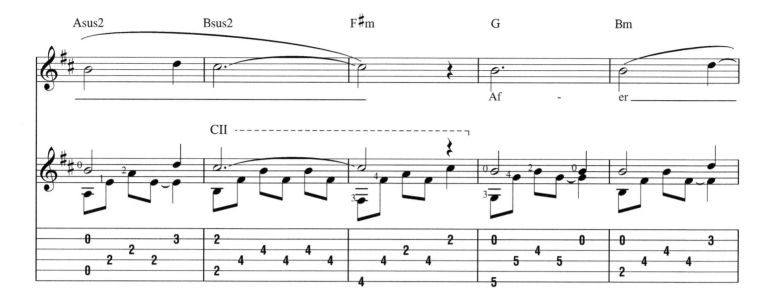

§ **Verse**

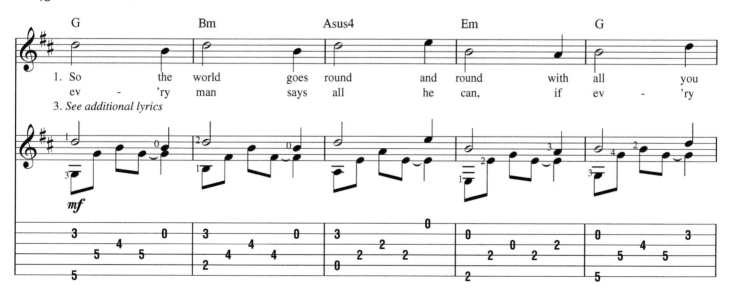

ev - er knew.
man - is true,

They say the sky
do I the be - lieve the

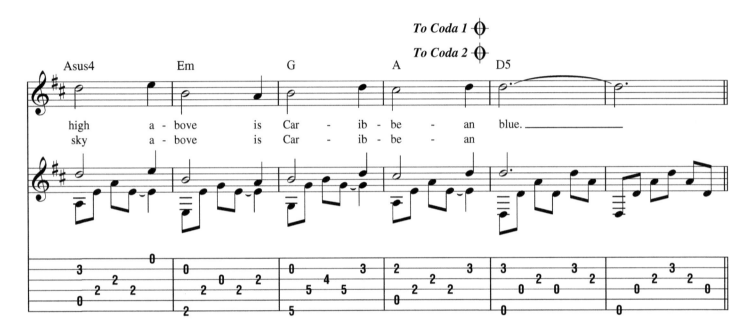

To Coda 1 ⊕
To Coda 2 ⊕

high a - bove is Car - ib - be - an blue. _____
sky a - bove is Car - ib - be - an

Interlude

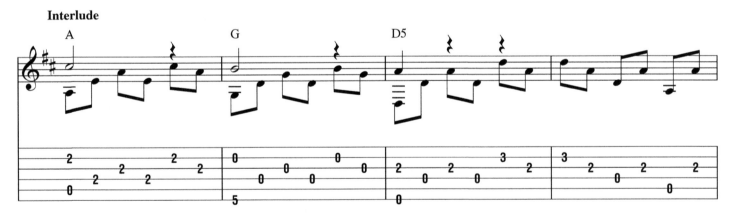

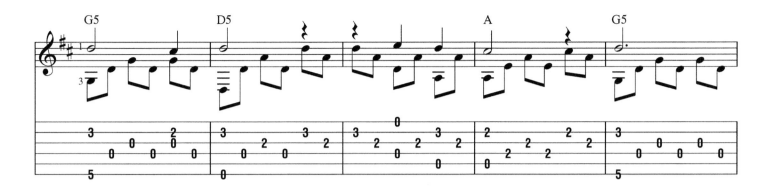

D.S. al Coda 1

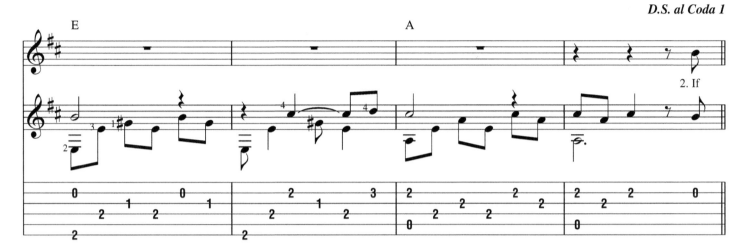

Coda 1　　　　　　　　　　　　　　**Interlude**

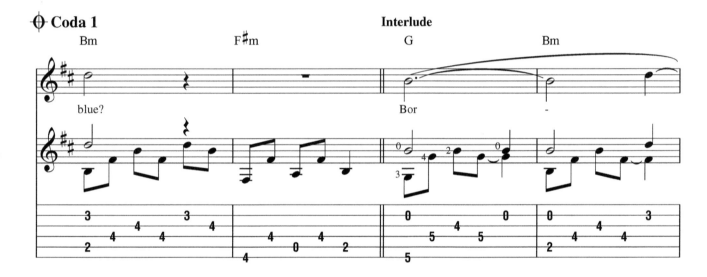

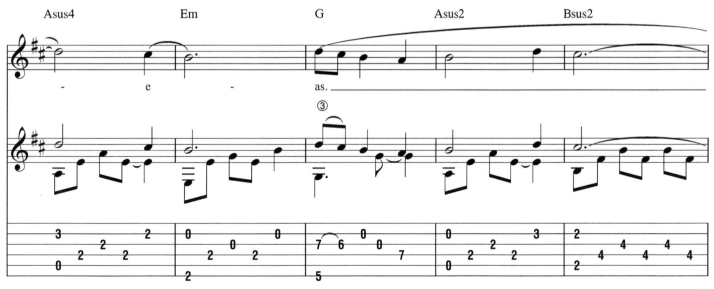

D.S. al Coda 2

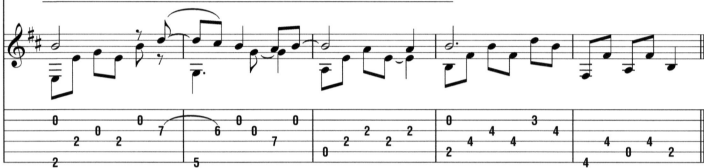

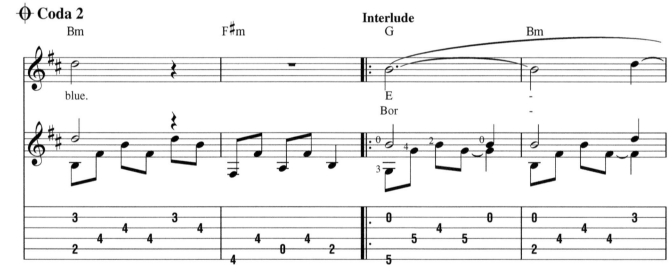

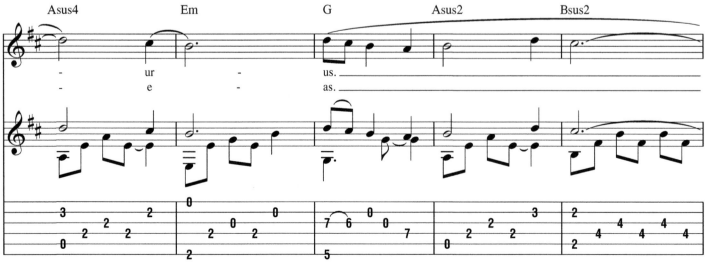

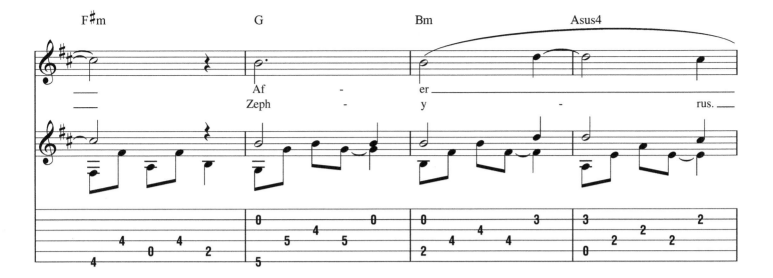

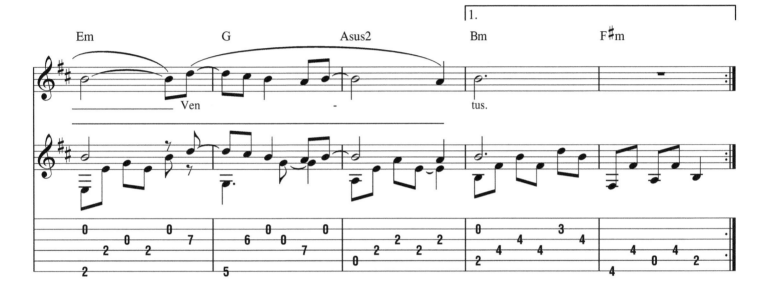

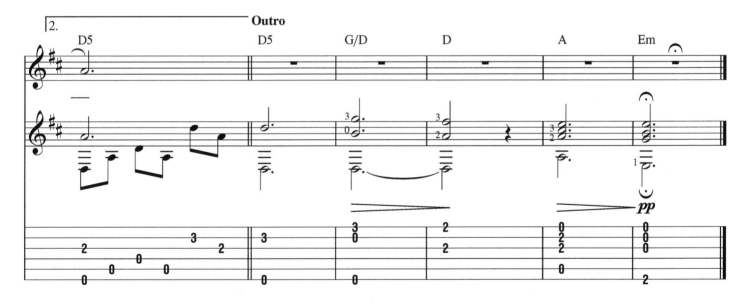

Additional Lyrics

3. If all you told was turned to gold,
   If all you dreamed was new,
   Imagine sky high above
   In Caribbean Blue.

China Roses

Words and Music by Enya, Nicky Ryan and Roma Ryan

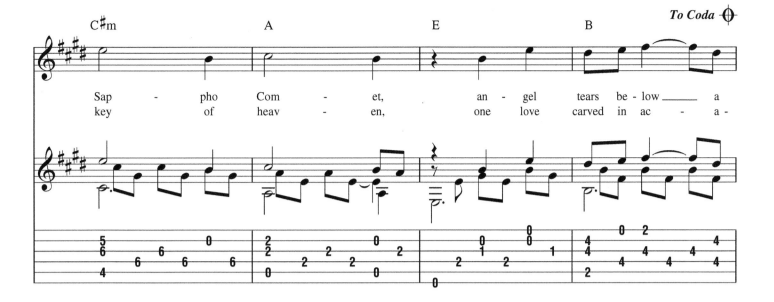

Sap - pho Com - et, an - gel tears be - low ____ a
key of heav - en, one love carved in ac - a -

Interlude

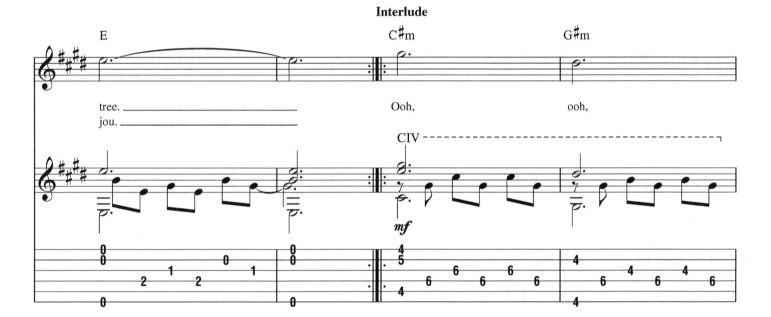

tree. ____ Ooh, ooh,
jou. ____

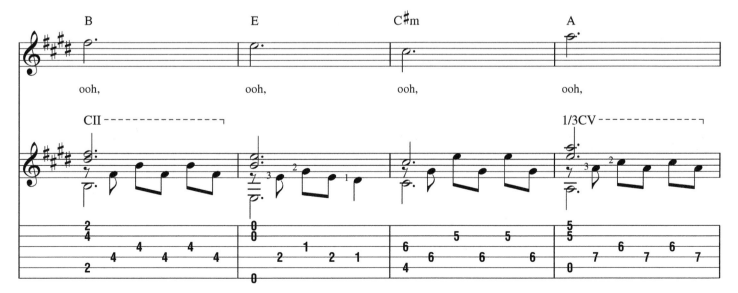

ooh, ooh, ooh, ooh,

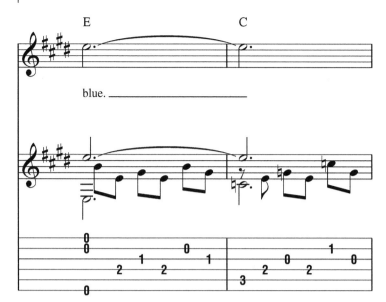

Bridge

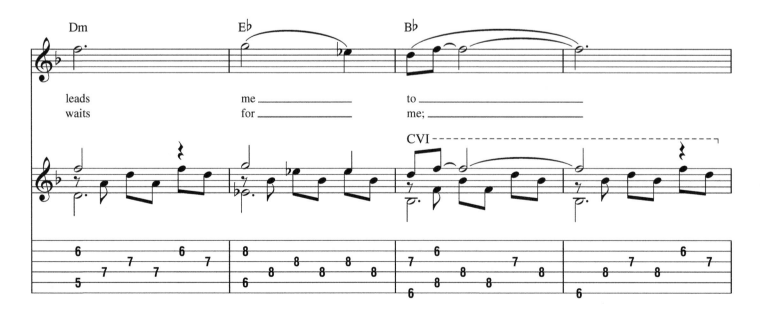

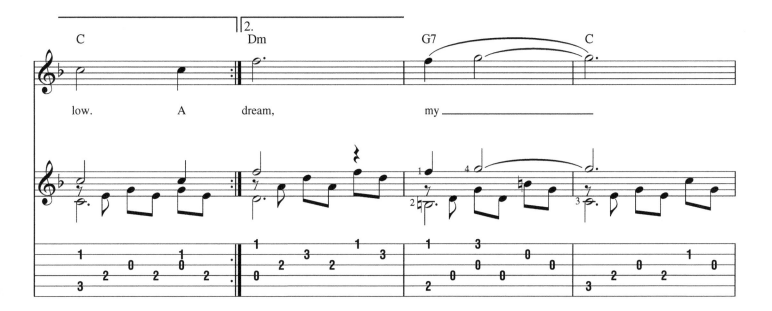

Verse

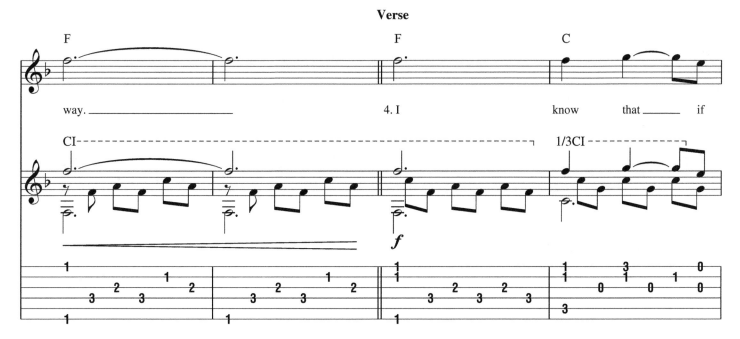

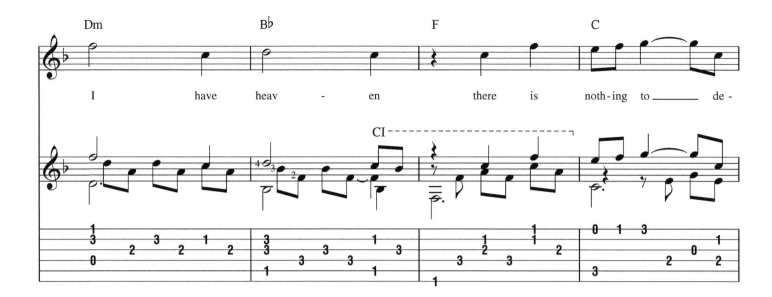

I have heav - en there is noth-ing to _____ de-

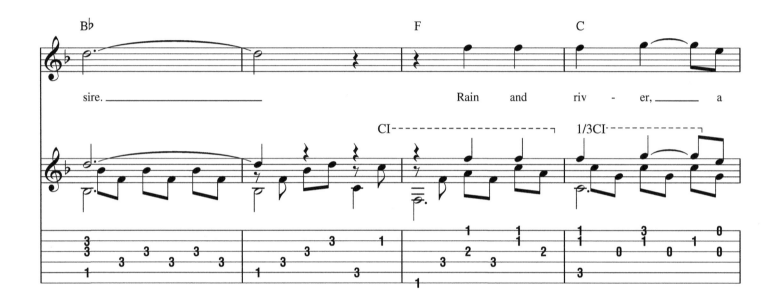

sire. _____ Rain and riv - er, _____ a

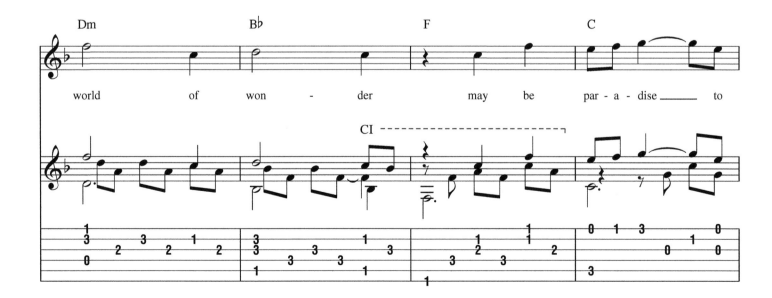

world of won - der may be par-a-dise _____ to

Outro

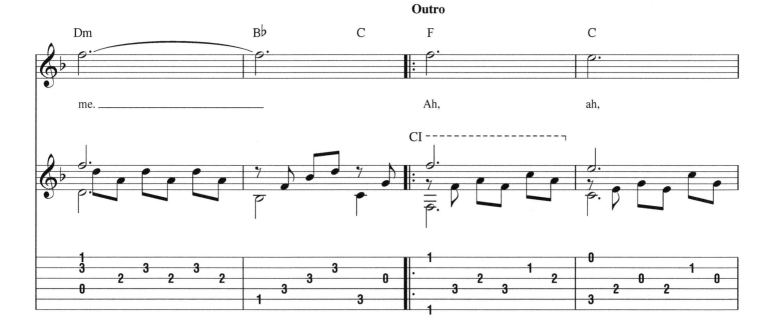

Additional Lyrics

3. One told me of china roses,
   One a thousand nights and one night,
   Earth's last picture, the end of evening:
   Hue of indigo and blue.

Fairytale

Written and Composed by Enya, Nicky Ryan and Roma Ryan

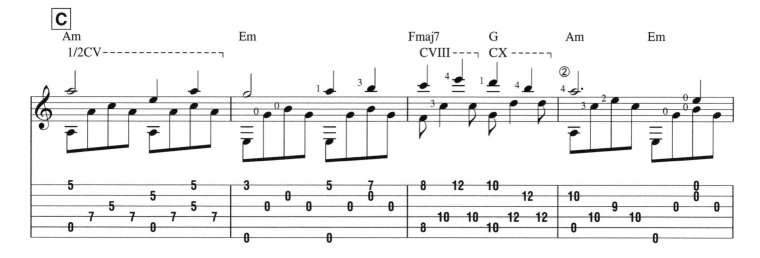

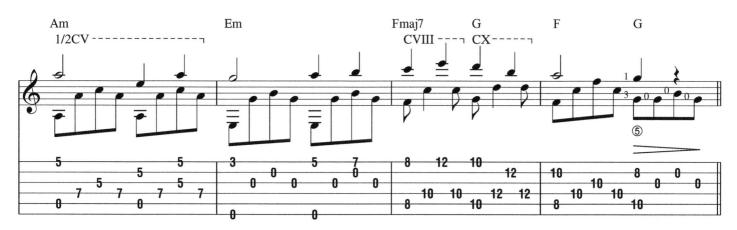

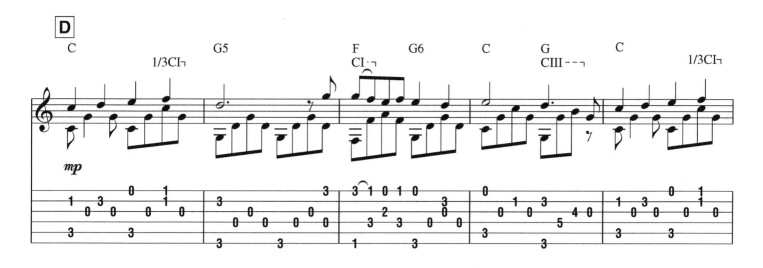

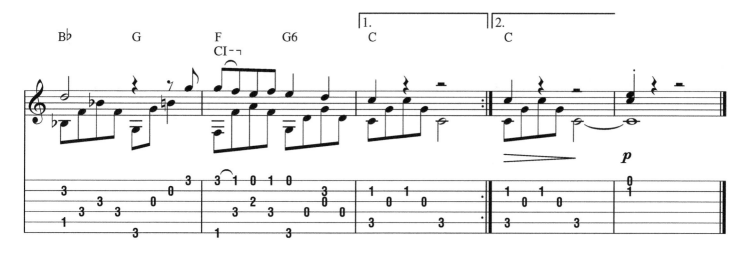

From Where I Am

By Enya and Nicky Ryan

Drop D tuning:
(low to high) D-A-D-G-B-E

Lothlorien

Composed and Arranged by Enya and Nicky Ryan

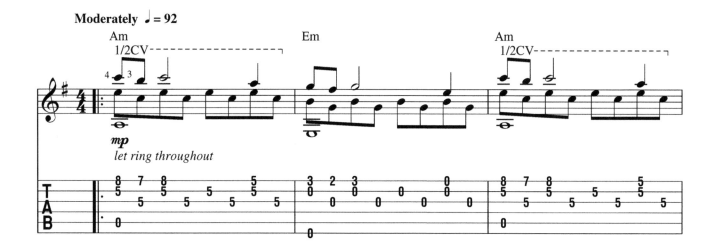

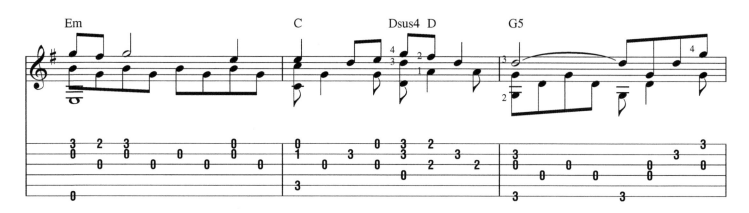

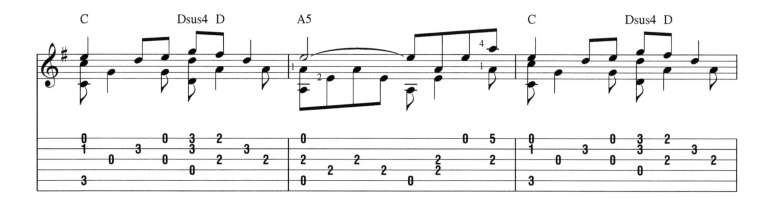

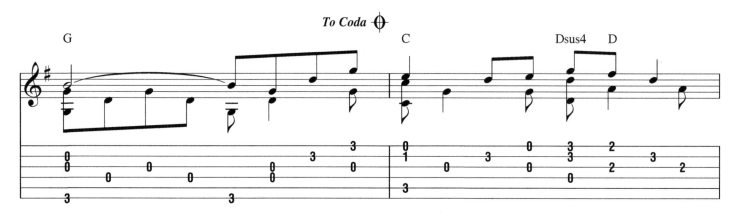

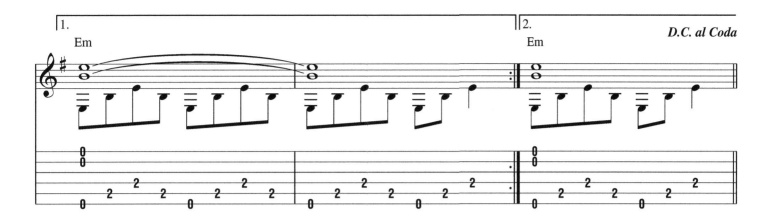

Coda

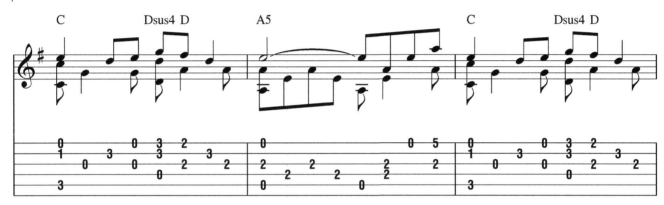

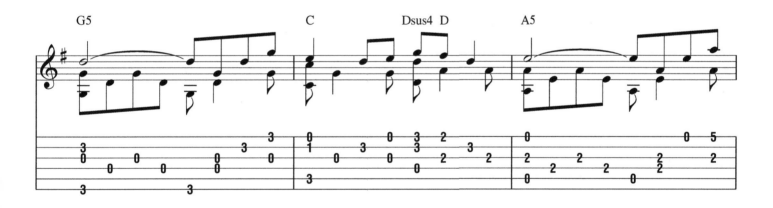

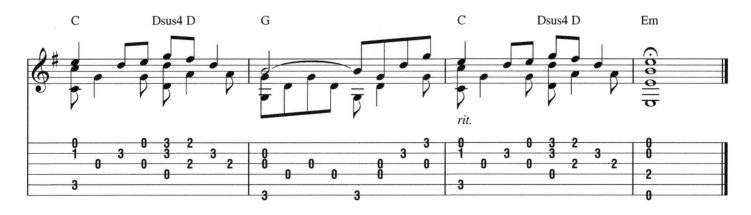

May It Be

from THE LORD OF THE RINGS: THE FELLOWSHIP OF THE RING
Words and Music by Enya, Nicky Ryan and Roma Ryan

Drop D tuning:
(low to high) D-A-D-G-B-E

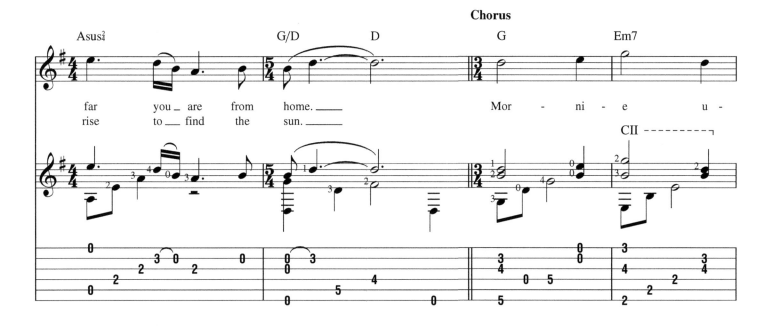

far   you   are   from   home.   Mor - ni - e   u -
rise   to   find   the   sun.

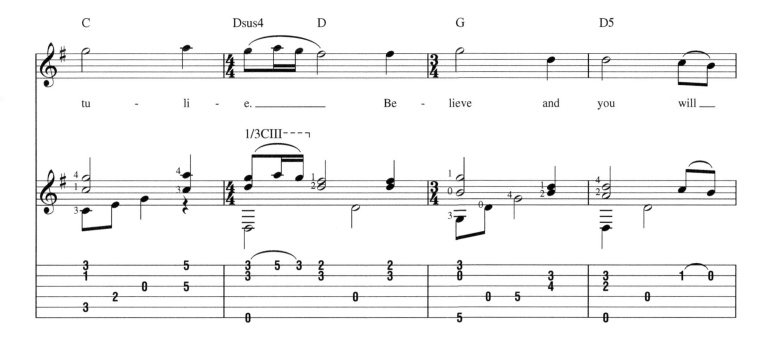

tu - li - e.   Be - lieve   and   you   will

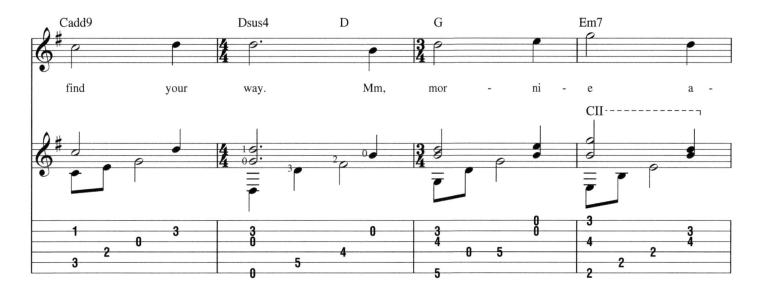

find   your   way.   Mm,   mor - ni - e   a -

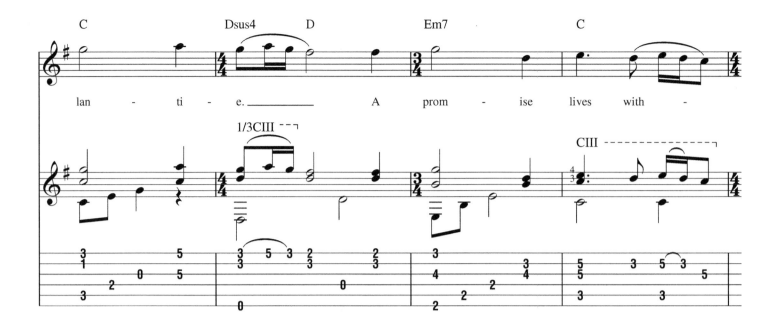

lan - ti - e._____ A prom - ise lives with -

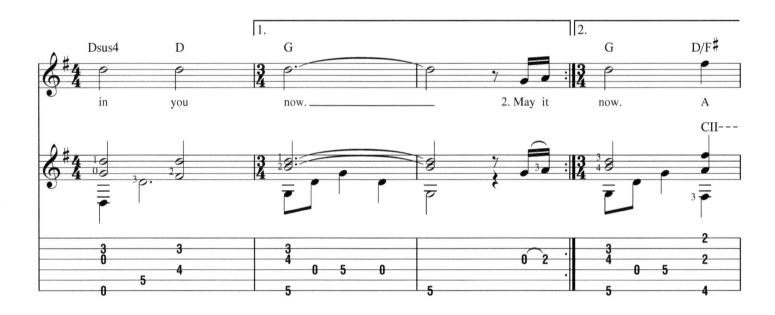

in you now._____ 2. May it now. A

prom - ise lives with - in you now.

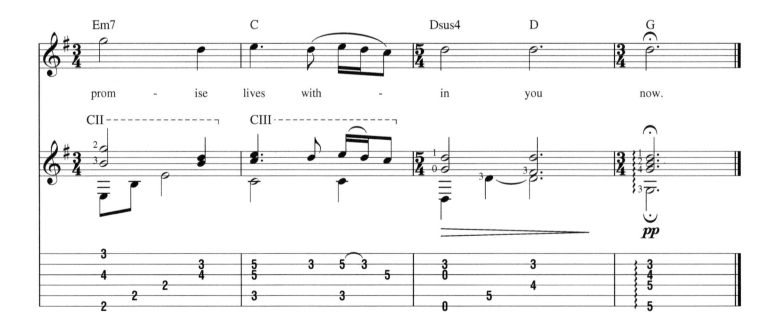

One by One

Words and Music by Enya, Nicky Ryan and Roma Ryan

Verse

1. Here am I yet an-oth-er good-bye.
2. It's no lie she is yearn-ing to fly.
3. *See additional lyrics*

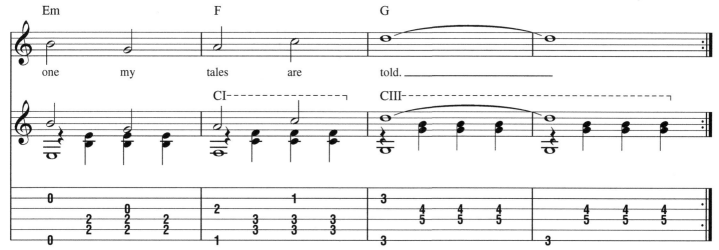

one   my   tales   are   told.

Coda

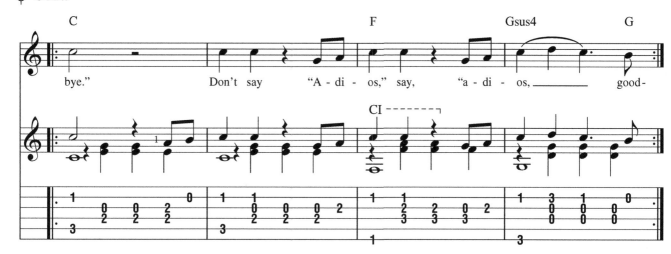

bye."   Don't   say   "A - di - os," say,   "a - di - os, _____   good-

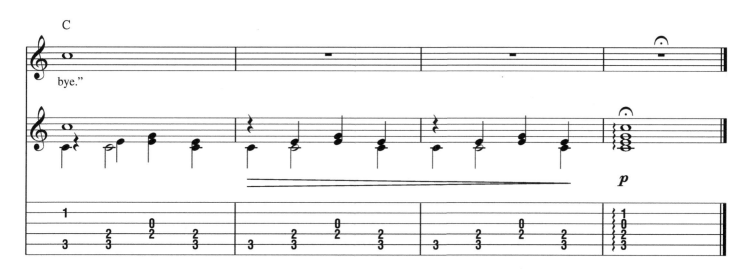

bye."

Additional Lyrics

3. No goodbyes
   For love brightens their eyes.
   Don't say, "Adios," say, "adios."
   And do you know why
   There's a love that won't die?
   Don't say, "Adios," say, "adios, goodbye."

No Holly for Miss Quinn

Composed and Arranged by Enya and Nicky Ryan

Drop D tuning:
(low to high) D-A-D-G-B-E

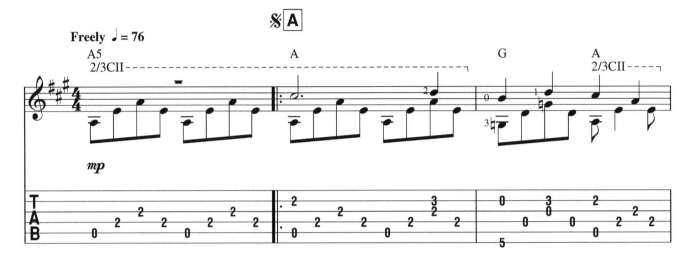

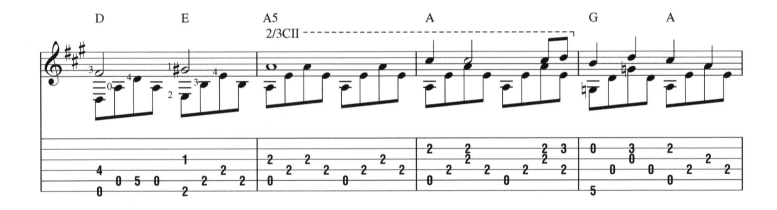

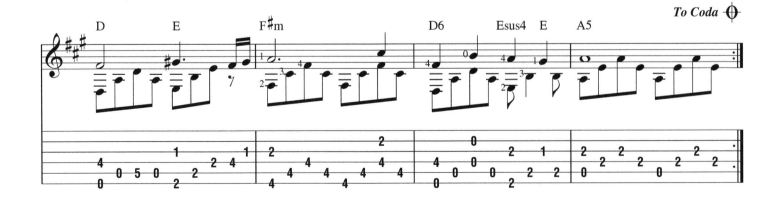

Only Time

from SWEET NOVEMBER

Words and Music by Enya, Nicky Ryan and Roma Ryan

Drop D tuning:
(low to high) D-A-D-G-B-E

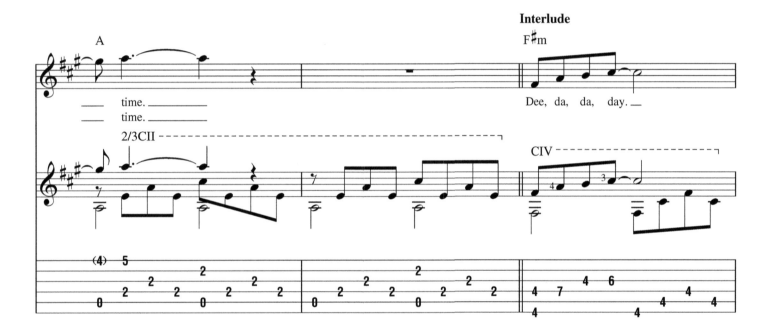

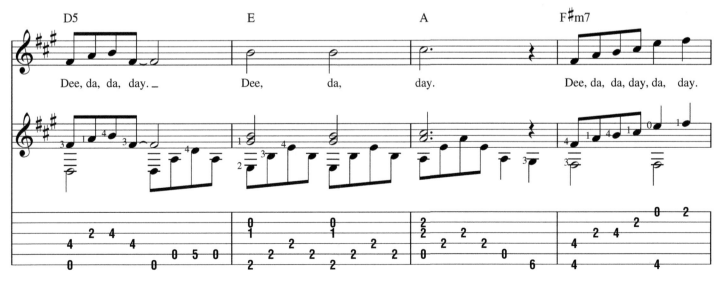

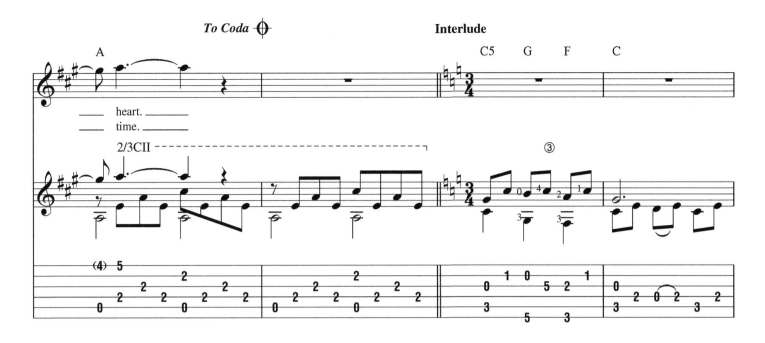

heart.
time.

Who knows? Only time.

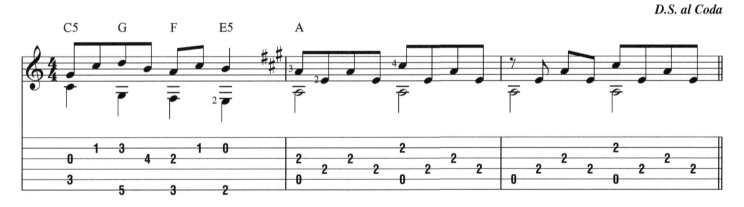

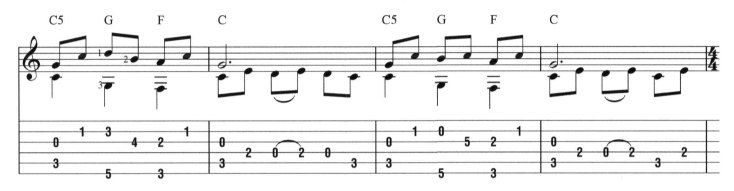

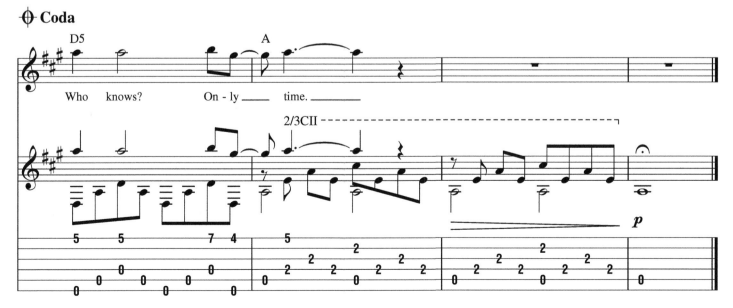

Pilgrim

Words and Music by Enya, Nicky Ryan and Roma Ryan

Drop D tuning:
(low to high) D-A-D-G-B-E

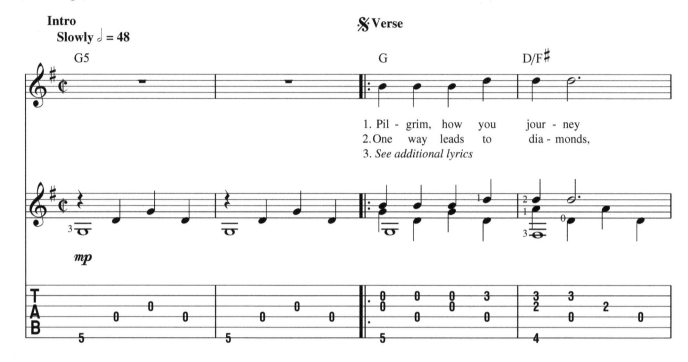

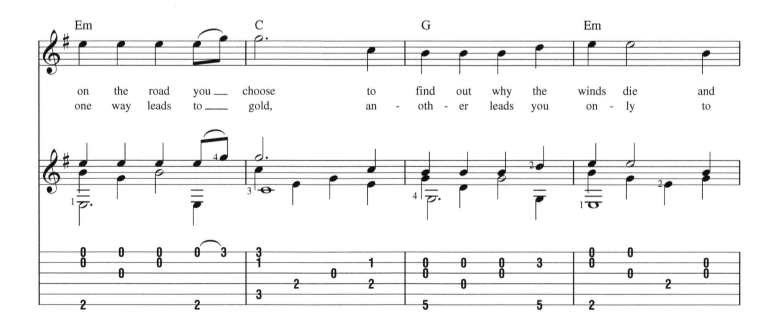

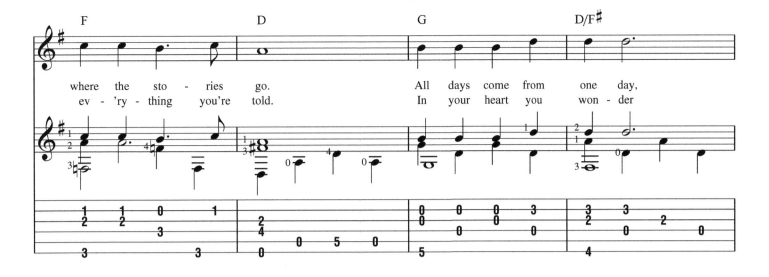

where the sto - ries go. All days come from one day,
ev - 'ry - thing you're told. In your heart you won - der

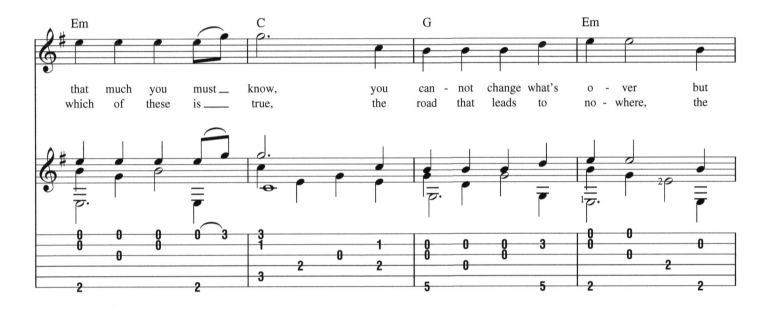

that much you must _ know, you can - not change what's o - ver but
which of these is _ true, the road that leads to no - where, the

To Coda ⊕ |1. |2.

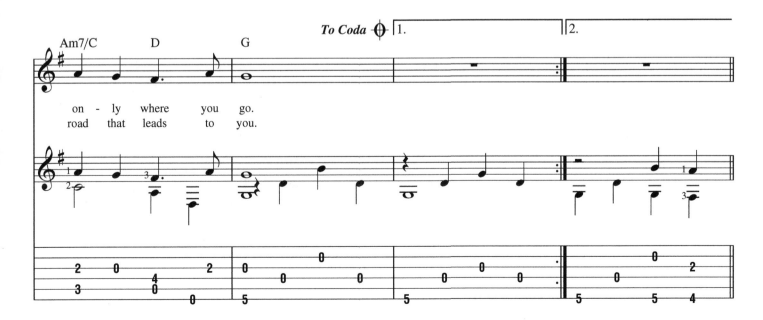

on - ly where you go.
road that leads to you.

Bridge

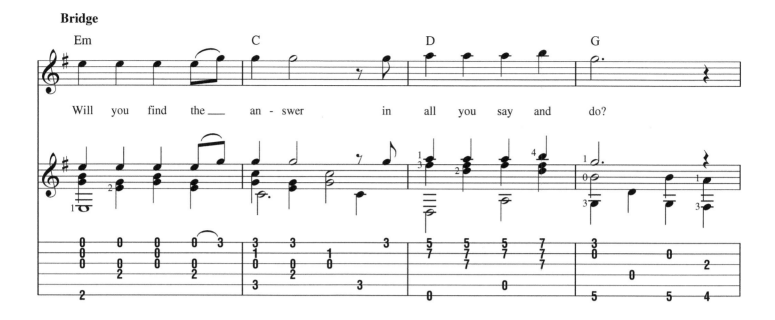

Will you find the ___ an - swer in all you say and do?

D.S. al Coda

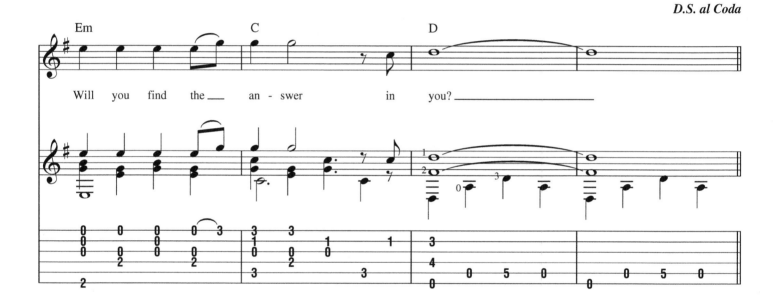

Will you find the ___ an - swer in you? _____

✠ **Coda**

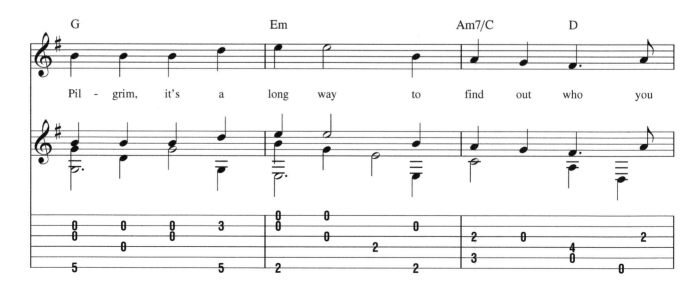

Pil - grim, it's a long way to find out who you

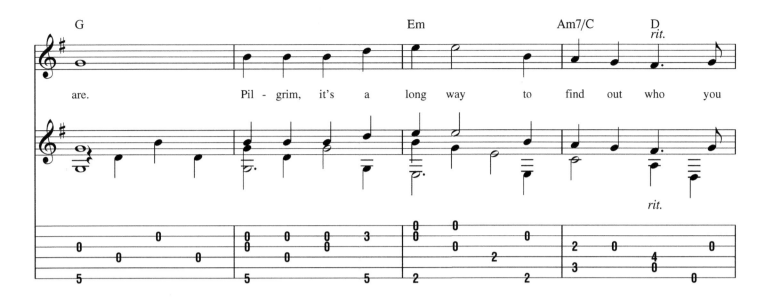

Pil - grim, it's a long way to find out who you are.

A tempo

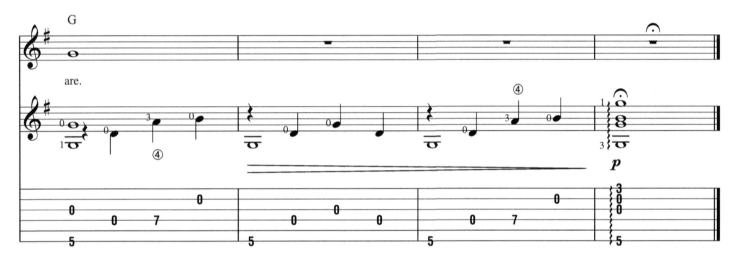

are.

Additional Lyrics

3. Each heart is a pilgrim, each one wants to know
   The reason why the winds die and where the stories go.
   Pilgrim, in your journey you may travel far,
   For pilgrim, it's a long way to find out who you are.

Portrait

Words and Music by Enya, Nicky Ryan and Roma Ryan

Drop D tuning:
(low to high) D-A-D-G-B-E

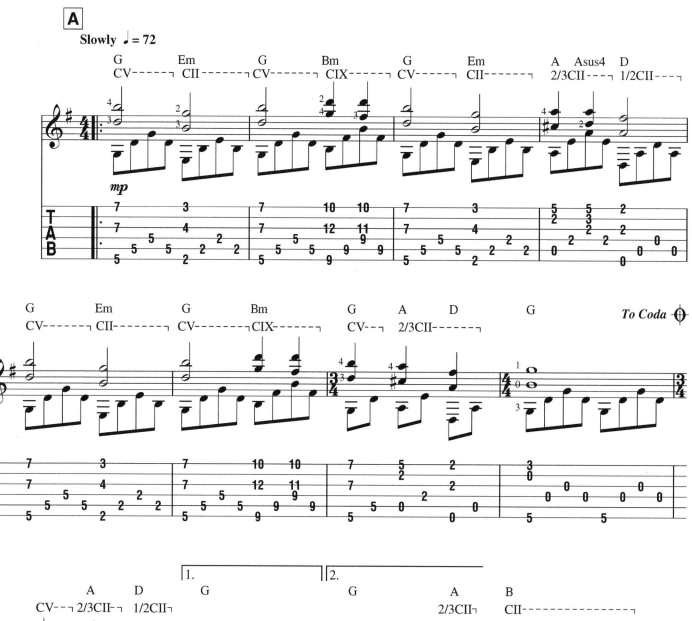

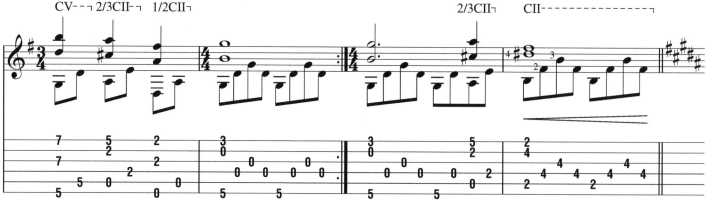

Watermark

Music by Enya
Words by Roma Ryan

Drop D tuning:
(low to high) D-A-D-G-B-E

Rubato ♩ = 63

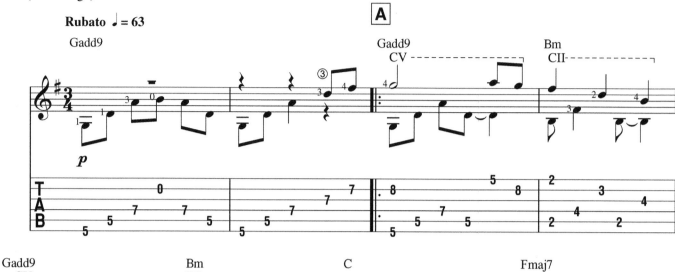

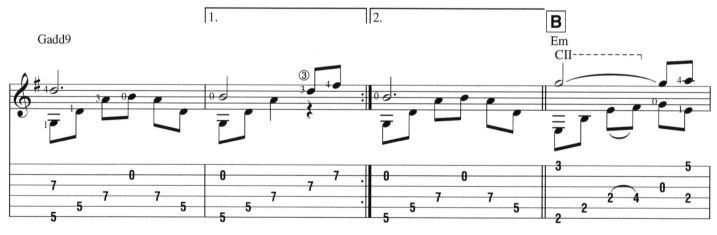

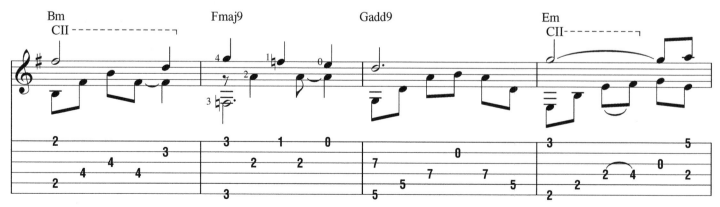

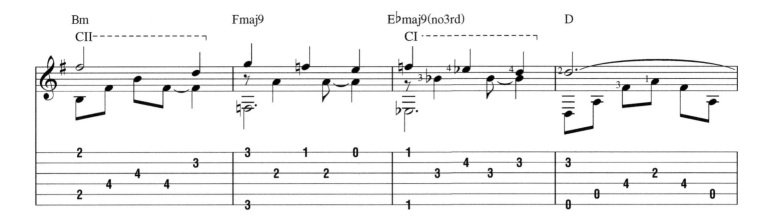

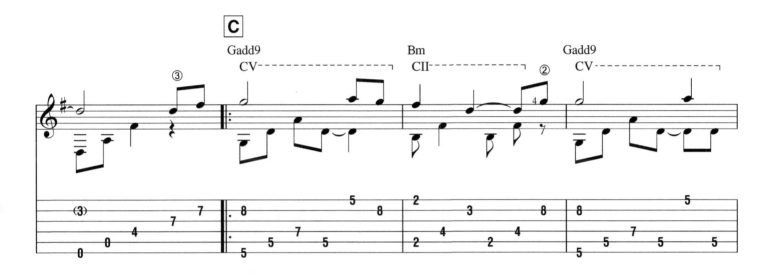

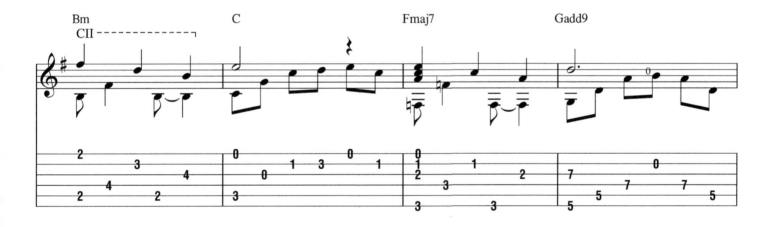

Story of Boadicea

Words and Music by Enya, Nicky Ryan and Roma Ryan

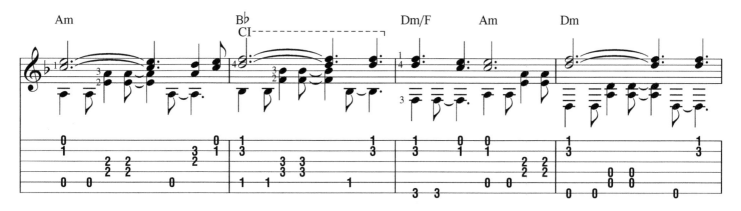

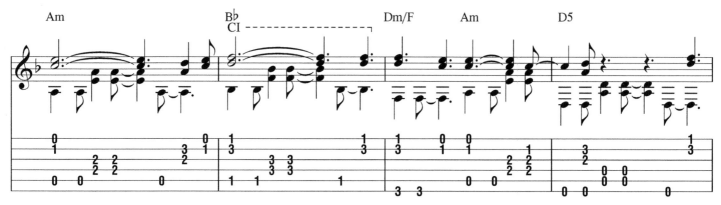

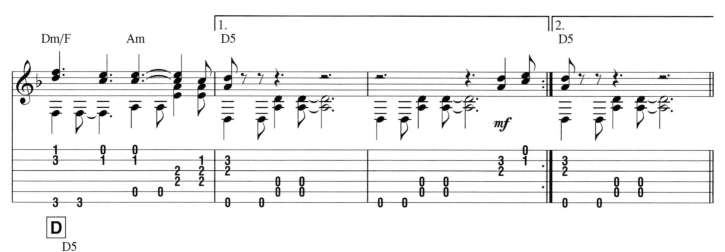

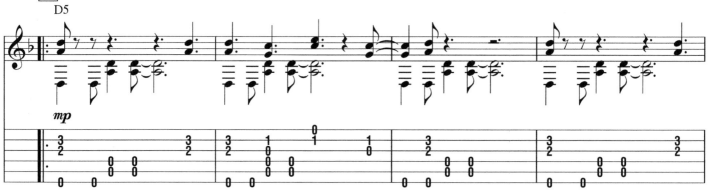

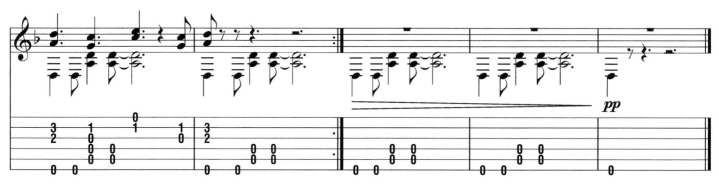

FINGERPICKING GUITAR BOOKS

Hone your fingerpicking skills with these great songbooks featuring solo guitar arrangements in standard notation and tablature. The arrangements in these books are carefully written for intermediate-level guitarists. Each song combines melody and harmony in one superb guitar fingerpicking arrangement. Each book also includes an introduction to basic fingerstyle guitar.

 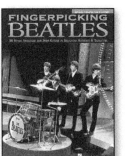 

Fingerpicking Acoustic
00699614 15 songs......................$14.99

Fingerpicking Acoustic Classics
00160211 15 songs......................$16.99

Fingerpicking Acoustic Hits
00160202 15 songs......................$12.99

Fingerpicking Acoustic Rock
00699764 14 songs......................$16.99

Fingerpicking Ballads
00699717 15 songs......................$14.99

Fingerpicking Beatles
00699049 30 songs......................$24.99

Fingerpicking Beethoven
00702390 15 pieces.....................$10.99

Fingerpicking Blues
00701277 15 songs $10.99

Fingerpicking Broadway Favorites
00699843 15 songs.....................$9.99

Fingerpicking Broadway Hits
00699838 15 songs.....................$7.99

Fingerpicking Campfire
00275964 15 songs......................$12.99

Fingerpicking Celtic Folk
00701148 15 songs......................$12.99

Fingerpicking Children's Songs
00699712 15 songs......................$9.99

Fingerpicking Christian
00701076 15 songs......................$12.99

Fingerpicking Christmas
00699599 20 carols......................$10.99

Fingerpicking Christmas Classics
00701695 15 songs.........................$7.99

Fingerpicking Christmas Songs
00171333 15 songs......................$10.99

Fingerpicking Classical
00699620 15 pieces.....................$10.99

Fingerpicking Country
00699687 17 songs......................$12.99

Fingerpicking Disney
00699711 15 songs......................$16.99

Fingerpicking Early Jazz Standards
00276565 15 songs $12.99

Fingerpicking Duke Ellington
00699845 15 songs.........................$9.99

Fingerpicking Enya
00701161 15 songs......................$16.99

Fingerpicking Film Score Music
00160143 15 songs......................$12.99

Fingerpicking Gospel
00701059 15 songs.......................$9.99

Fingerpicking Hit Songs
00160195 15 songs......................$12.99

Fingerpicking Hymns
00699688 15 hymns $12.99

Fingerpicking Irish Songs
00701965 15 songs......................$10.99

Fingerpicking Italian Songs
00159778 15 songs......................$12.99

Fingerpicking Jazz Favorites
00699844 15 songs......................$12.99

Fingerpicking Jazz Standards
00699840 15 songs......................$12.99

Fingerpicking Elton John
00237495 15 songs......................$14.99

Fingerpicking Latin Favorites
00699842 15 songs......................$12.99

Fingerpicking Latin Standards
00699837 15 songs......................$17.99

Fingerpicking Andrew Lloyd Webber
00699839 14 songs......................$16.99

Fingerpicking Love Songs
00699841 15 songs......................$14.99

Fingerpicking Love Standards
00699836 15 songs $9.99

Fingerpicking Lullabyes
00701276 16 songs.........................$9.99

Fingerpicking Movie Music
00699919 15 songs......................$14.99

Fingerpicking Mozart
00699794 15 pieces.....................$10.99

Fingerpicking Pop
00699615 15 songs......................$14.99

Fingerpicking Popular Hits
00139079 14 songs......................$12.99

Fingerpicking Praise
00699714 15 songs......................$14.99

Fingerpicking Rock
00699716 15 songs......................$14.99

Fingerpicking Standards
00699613 17 songs......................$14.99

Fingerpicking Wedding
00699637 15 songs......................$10.99

Fingerpicking Worship
00700554 15 songs......................$14.99

Fingerpicking Neil Young – Greatest Hits
00700134 16 songs......................$16.99

Fingerpicking Yuletide
00699654 16 songs......................$12.99

HAL•LEONARD®

Order these and more great publications from your favorite music retailer at
halleonard.com

Prices, contents and availability subject to change without notice.

AUTHENTIC CHORDS • ORIGINAL KEYS • COMPLETE SONGS

The *Strum It* series lets players strum the chords and sing along with their favorite hits. Each song has been selected because it can be played with regular open chords, barre chords, or other moveable chord types. Guitarists can simply play the rhythm, or play and sing along through the entire song. All songs are shown in their original keys complete with chords, strum patterns, melody and lyrics. Wherever possible, the chord voicings from the recorded versions are notated.

THE BEACH BOYS' GREATEST HITS
00699357......................... $12.95

THE BEATLES FAVORITES
00699249.........................$15.99

VERY BEST OF JOHNNY CASH
00699514.........................$14.99

CELTIC GUITAR SONGBOOK
00699265.........................$12.99

CHRISTMAS SONGS FOR GUITAR
00699247.........................$10.95

CHRISTMAS SONGS WITH 3 CHORDS
00699487.........................$9.99

VERY BEST OF ERIC CLAPTON
00699560.........................$12.95

JIM CROCE – CLASSIC HITS
00699269.........................$10.95

DISNEY FAVORITES
00699171.........................$14.99

MELISSA ETHERIDGE GREATEST HITS
00699518.........................$12.99

FAVORITE SONGS WITH 3 CHORDS
00699112.........................$10.99

FAVORITE SONGS WITH 4 CHORDS
00699270.........................$8.95

FIRESIDE SING-ALONG
00699273.........................$12.99

FOLK FAVORITES
00699517.........................$8.95

THE GUITAR STRUMMERS' ROCK SONGBOOK
00701678.........................$14.99

BEST OF WOODY GUTHRIE
00699496.........................$12.95

JOHN HIATT COLLECTION
00699398.........................$17.99

THE VERY BEST OF BOB MARLEY
00699524.........................$14.99

A MERRY CHRISTMAS SONGBOOK
00699211.........................$10.99

MORE FAVORITE SONGS WITH 3 CHORDS
00699532.........................$9.99

THE VERY BEST OF TOM PETTY
00699336.........................$15.99

BEST OF GEORGE STRAIT
00699235.........................$16.99

TAYLOR SWIFT FOR ACOUSTIC GUITAR
00109717.........................$16.99

BEST OF HANK WILLIAMS JR.
00699224.........................$16.99

HAL•LEONARD®

Prices, contents & availability subject to change without notice.

Visit Hal Leonard online at
www.halleonard.com

0319
134

PLAY THE CLASSICS

JAZZ FOLIOS FOR GUITARISTS

BEST OF JAZZ GUITAR

by Wolf Marshall • Signature Licks

In this book/audio pack, Wolf Marshall provides a hands-on analysis of 10 of the most frequently played tunes in the jazz genre, as played by the leading guitarists of all time. Features: All the Things You Are • How Insensitive • I'll Remember April • So What • Yesterdays • and more.

00695586 Book/Online Audio $29.99

GUITAR STANDARDS

Classic Jazz Masters Series

16 classic jazz guitar performances transcribed note for note with tablature: All of You (Kenny Burrell) • Easter Parade (Herb Ellis) • I'll Remember April (Grant Green) • Lover Man (Django Reinhardt) • Song for My Father (George Benson) • The Way You Look Tonight (Wes Montgomery) • and more. Includes a discography.

00699143 Guitar Transcriptions $14.95

JAZZ CLASSICS FOR SOLO GUITAR

arranged by Robert B. Yelin

This collection includes excellent chord melody arrangements in standard notation and tablature for 35 all-time jazz favorites: April in Paris • Cry Me a River • Day by Day • God Bless' the Child • It Might as Well Be Spring • Lover • My Romance • Nuages • Satin Doll • Tenderly • Unchained Melody • Wave • and more!

00699279 Solo Guitar $19.99

JAZZ FAVORITES FOR SOLO GUITAR

arranged by Robert B. Yelin

This fantastic 35-song collection includes lush chord melody arrangements in standard notation and tab: Autumn in New York • Call Me Irresponsible • How Deep Is the Ocean • I Could Write a Book • The Lady Is a Tramp • Mood Indigo • Polka Dots and Moonbeams • Solitude • Take the "A" Train • Where or When • more.

00699278 Solo Guitar $19.99

JAZZ GEMS FOR SOLO GUITAR

arranged by Robert B. Yelin

35 great solo arrangements of jazz classics, including: After You've Gone • Alice in Wonderland • The Christmas Song • Four • Meditation • Stompin' at the Savoy • Sweet and Lovely • Waltz for Debby • Yardbird Suite • You'll Never Walk Alone • You've Changed • and more.

00699617 Solo Guitar $19.99

JAZZ GUITAR BIBLE

The one book that has all of the jazz guitar classics transcribed note-for-note, with standard notation and tablature. Includes over 30 songs: Body and Soul • Girl Talk • I'll Remember April • In a Sentimental Mood • My Funny Valentine • Nuages • Satin Doll • So What • Stardust • Take Five • Tangerine • Yardbird Suite • and more.

00690466 Guitar Recorded Versions $27.99

JAZZ GUITAR CHORD MELODIES

arranged & performed by Dan Towey

This book/CD pack includes complete solo performances of 12 standards, including: All the Things You Are • Body and Soul • My Romance • How Insensitive • My One and Only Love • and more. The arrangements are performance level and range in difficulty from intermediate to advanced.

00698988 Book/CD Pack $19.95

JAZZ GUITAR PLAY-ALONG

Guitar Play-Along Volume 16

With this book/audio pack, all you have to do is follow the tab, listen to the online audio to hear how the guitar should sound, and then play along using the separate backing tracks. 8 songs: All Blues • Bluesette • Footprints • How Insensitive (Insensatez) • Misty • Satin Doll • Stella by Starlight • Tenor Madness.

00699584 Book/Online Audio $16.99

JAZZ STANDARDS FOR FINGERSTYLE GUITAR

20 songs, including: All the Things You Are • Autumn Leaves • Bluesette • Body and Soul • Fly Me to the Moon • The Girl from Ipanema • How Insensitive • I've Grown Accustomed to Her Face • My Funny Valentine • Satin Doll • Stompin' at the Savoy • and more.

00699029 Fingerstyle Guitar $17.99

JAZZ STANDARDS FOR SOLO GUITAR

arranged by Robert B. Yelin

35 chord melody guitar arrangements, including: Ain't Misbehavin' • Autumn Leaves • Bewitched • Cherokee • Darn That Dream • Girl Talk • I've Got You Under My Skin • Lullaby of Birdland • My Funny Valentine • A Nightingale Sang in Berkeley Square • Stella by Starlight • The Very Thought of You • and more.

00699277 Solo Guitar $19.99

101 MUST-KNOW JAZZ LICKS

by Wolf Marshall

Add a jazz feel and flavor to your playing! 101 definitive licks, plus demonstration audio, from every major jazz guitar style, neatly organized into easy-to-use categories. They're all here: swing and pre-bop, bebop, post-bop modern jazz, hard bop and cool jazz, modal jazz, soul jazz and postmodern jazz.

00695433 Book/Online Audio $19.99

HAL•LEONARD®

Visit Hal Leonard Online at **www.halleonard.com**

Prices, contents and availability subject to change without notice.

EASY GUITAR WITH NOTES & TAB

This series features simplified arrangements with notes, tab, chord charts, and strum and pick patterns.

MIXED FOLIOS

00702287	Acoustic	$19.99
00702002	Acoustic Rock Hits for Easy Guitar	$15.99
00702166	All-Time Best Guitar Collection	$19.99
00702232	Best Acoustic Songs for Easy Guitar	$16.99
00119835	Best Children's Songs	$16.99
00703055	The Big Book of Nursery Rhymes & Children's Songs	$16.99
00698978	Big Christmas Collection	$19.99
00702394	Bluegrass Songs for Easy Guitar	$15.99
00289632	Bohemian Rhapsody	$19.99
00703387	Celtic Classics	$16.99
00224808	Chart Hits of 2016-2017	$14.99
00267383	Chart Hits of 2017-2018	$14.99
00334293	Chart Hits of 2019-2020	$16.99
00403479	Chart Hits of 2021-2022	$16.99
00702149	Children's Christian Songbook	$9.99
00702028	Christmas Classics	$8.99
00101779	Christmas Guitar	$14.99
00702141	Classic Rock	$8.95
00159642	Classical Melodies	$12.99
00253933	Disney/Pixar's Coco	$16.99
00702203	CMT's 100 Greatest Country Songs	$34.99
00702283	The Contemporary Christian Collection	$16.99

00196954	Contemporary Disney	$19.99
00702239	Country Classics for Easy Guitar	$24.99
00702257	Easy Acoustic Guitar Songs	$17.99
00702041	Favorite Hymns for Easy Guitar	$12.99
00222701	Folk Pop Songs	$17.99
00126894	Frozen	$14.99
00333922	Frozen 2	$14.99
00702286	Glee	$16.99
00702160	The Great American Country Songbook	$19.99
00702148	Great American Gospel for Guitar	$14.99
00702050	Great Classical Themes for Easy Guitar	$9.99
00275088	The Greatest Showman	$17.99
00148030	Halloween Guitar Songs	$14.99
00702273	Irish Songs	$14.99
00192503	Jazz Classics for Easy Guitar	$16.99
00702275	Jazz Favorites for Easy Guitar	$17.99
00702274	Jazz Standards for Easy Guitar	$19.99
00702162	Jumbo Easy Guitar Songbook	$24.99
00232285	La La Land	$16.99
00702258	Legends of Rock	$14.99
00702189	MTV's 100 Greatest Pop Songs	$34.99
00702272	1950s Rock	$16.99
00702271	1960s Rock	$16.99
00702270	1970s Rock	$24.99
00702269	1980s Rock	$16.99

00702268	1990s Rock	$24.99
00369043	Rock Songs for Kids	$14.99
00109725	Once	$14.99
00702187	Selections from O Brother Where Art Thou?	$19.99
00702178	100 Songs for Kids	$16.99
00702515	Pirates of the Caribbean	$17.99
00702125	Praise and Worship for Guitar	$14.99
00287930	Songs from *A Star Is Born, The Greatest Showman, La La Land*, and More Movie Musicals	$16.99
00702285	Southern Rock Hits	$12.99
00156420	Star Wars Music	$16.99
00121535	30 Easy Celtic Guitar Solos	$16.99
00244654	Top Hits of 2017	$14.99
00283786	Top Hits of 2018	$14.99
00302269	Top Hits of 2019	$14.99
00355779	Top Hits of 2020	$14.99
00374083	Top Hits of 2021	$16.99
00702294	Top Worship Hits	$17.99
00702255	VH1's 100 Greatest Hard Rock Songs	$34.99
00702175	VH1's 100 Greatest Songs of Rock and Roll	$34.99
00702253	Wicked	$12.99

ARTIST COLLECTIONS

00702267	AC/DC for Easy Guitar	$16.99
00156221	Adele – 25	$16.99
00396889	Adele – 30	$19.99
00702040	Best of the Allman Brothers	$16.99
00702865	J.S. Bach for Easy Guitar	$15.99
00702169	Best of The Beach Boys	$16.99
00702292	The Beatles — 1	$22.99
00125796	Best of Chuck Berry	$16.99
00702201	The Essential Black Sabbath	$15.99
00702250	blink-182 — Greatest Hits	$17.99
02501615	Zac Brown Band — The Foundation	$17.99
02501621	Zac Brown Band — You Get What You Give	$16.99
00702043	Best of Johnny Cash	$17.99
00702090	Eric Clapton's Best	$16.99
00702086	Eric Clapton — from the Album Unplugged	$17.99
00702202	The Essential Eric Clapton	$17.99
00702053	Best of Patsy Cline	$17.99
00222697	Very Best of Coldplay – 2nd Edition	$17.99
00702229	The Very Best of Creedence Clearwater Revival	$16.99
00702145	Best of Jim Croce	$16.99
00702278	Crosby, Stills & Nash	$12.99
14042809	Bob Dylan	$15.99
00702276	Fleetwood Mac — Easy Guitar Collection	$17.99
00139462	The Very Best of Grateful Dead	$16.99
00702136	Best of Merle Haggard	$16.99
00702227	Jimi Hendrix — Smash Hits	$19.99
00702288	Best of Hillsong United	$12.99
00702236	Best of Antonio Carlos Jobim	$15.99

00702245	Elton John — Greatest Hits 1970–2002	$19.99
00129855	Jack Johnson	$17.99
00702204	Robert Johnson	$16.99
00702234	Selections from Toby Keith — 35 Biggest Hits	$12.95
00702003	Kiss	$16.99
00702216	Lynyrd Skynyrd	$17.99
00702182	The Essential Bob Marley	$16.99
00146081	Maroon 5	$14.99
00121925	Bruno Mars – Unorthodox Jukebox	$12.99
00702248	Paul McCartney — All the Best	$14.99
00125484	The Best of MercyMe	$12.99
00702209	Steve Miller Band — Young Hearts (Greatest Hits)	$12.95
00124167	Jason Mraz	$15.99
00702096	Best of Nirvana	$16.99
00702211	The Offspring — Greatest Hits	$17.99
00138026	One Direction	$17.99
00702030	Best of Roy Orbison	$17.99
00702144	Best of Ozzy Osbourne	$14.99
00702279	Tom Petty	$17.99
00102911	Pink Floyd	$17.99
00702139	Elvis Country Favorites	$19.99
00702293	The Very Best of Prince	$19.99
00699415	Best of Queen for Guitar	$16.99
00109279	Best of R.E.M.	$14.99
00702208	Red Hot Chili Peppers — Greatest Hits	$17.99
00198960	The Rolling Stones	$17.99
00174793	The Very Best of Santana	$16.99
00702196	Best of Bob Seger	$16.99
00146046	Ed Sheeran	$17.99

00702252	Frank Sinatra — Nothing But the Best	$12.99
00702010	Best of Rod Stewart	$17.99
00702049	Best of George Strait	$17.99
00702259	Taylor Swift for Easy Guitar	$15.99
00359800	Taylor Swift – Easy Guitar Anthology	$24.99
00702260	Taylor Swift — Fearless	$14.99
00139727	Taylor Swift — 1989	$19.99
00115960	Taylor Swift — Red	$16.99
00253667	Taylor Swift — Reputation	$17.99
00702290	Taylor Swift — Speak Now	$16.99
00232849	Chris Tomlin Collection – 2nd Edition	$14.99
00702226	Chris Tomlin — See the Morning	$12.95
00148643	Train	$14.99
00702427	U2 — 18 Singles	$19.99
00702108	Best of Stevie Ray Vaughan	$17.99
00279005	The Who	$14.99
00702123	Best of Hank Williams	$15.99
00194548	Best of John Williams	$14.99
00702228	Neil Young — Greatest Hits	$17.99
00119133	Neil Young — Harvest	$14.99

Prices, contents and availability subject to change without notice.

HAL•LEONARD®

Visit Hal Leonard online at halleonard.com